# Harvest Festivals

## Gare Thompson

# Contents

# Celebrating a Good Crop

People all over the world celebrate after crops are harvested. Farming is hard work. First, farmers plow their fields. Then, they plant the seeds and wait for them to grow. They water the plants and hope for rain, too. Water helps the crops grow.

A farmer uses a machine to plant corn seeds.

After months of hard work, it is time to harvest the crops. Farmers sweat as they cut the wheat, pull up the yams, and pick the corn.

The hard work is done. Now it is time to celebrate. The farmers have a festival. Most harvest festivals include singing, dancing, giving thanks, and, of course, lots of good food.

The corn in this field is ready to be harvested.

5

# Celebrating Holi

People in India celebrate the festival of Holi in March. This festival takes place after the wheat harvest. Wheat is an important crop. It is used to make flour, bread, cereal, and other foods.

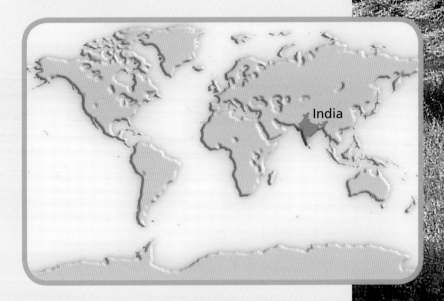

India

These workers in India gather wheat by hand.

People light bonfires the night before Holi begins. According to legend, long ago a king wanted to be worshipped like a god. But the king's son, Prahlad, chose to worship the god Vishnu. This made the king very angry. He ordered Prahlad to be killed. Prahlad's evil sister, Holika, led Prahlad into a bonfire. Everyone thought Prahlad would die. Vishnu saved Prahlad. Holika died instead. The festival of Holi is named after Holika. The bonfires remind people that good wins over evil.

The Holi festival begins with a bonfire.

Holi is a favorite festival of the children. During the festival, everyone dusts themselves with brightly colored powders. The colored powders are called *gulal*. Then, people squirt each other with water. Soon, everyone is covered with bright colors.

Children celebrate Holi by coloring each other with *gulal*.

The custom of coloring people with bright colors came from a story about the god, Krishna. According to the story, Krishna liked playing tricks on his friend, Radha, and her friends. He often soaked them in colored water. Then, when Radha and her friends were getting cleaned up, Krishna hid their clothes.

This painting shows Krishna with his friend, Radha.

# Holi Rang Lemonade

Make this Holi festival drink and have a colorful celebration with your friends!

## You will need:

- Ice cube trays
- Cups
- Red, green, and yellow food coloring
- Lemonade
- Canned fruit
- Slices of lemon

## What to do:

1. Fill the ice cube trays with water.
2. Make different-colored ice cubes by adding food coloring to the water in the trays.
3. Freeze the ice cube trays.
4. Put a spoonful of fruit and colored ice cubes into a cup.
5. Pour in the lemonade.
6. Put a slice of lemon on the rim of the cup.

# Celebrating the Yam Festival

Ghana is a country in Africa. People here celebrate the yam festival in the fall. This festival celebrates the yam harvest. Yams are an important crop in Ghana. They can be boiled or roasted. They can also be made into flour.

Ghana

Farmers in Ghana dig yams out of the ground.

The yam festival lasts a week. It is a time when farmers honor the gods that watched over their crops. The festival begins with a cleaning ceremony. A group of people wash special stools to honor family members who have died. Roads to the village are blocked to prevent evil spirits from entering.

The festival begins with a cleaning ceremony.

Farmers carry yams to the village on their heads.

In the forest, the first yams are taken from the ground. The farmers carry the yams to the village. The yams are then blessed and given to the chief. The chief has them cooked and shares them with everyone in the village.

The festival ends with a huge feast. Everyone gathers in the center of the village to sing, dance, and eat. Drummers beat their drums loudly. The new yams are paraded in front of the chiefs and the villagers. People give thanks and enjoy the newly harvested yams.

Villagers carry stools on their heads. The stools honor those who have died.

# Yam Fufu Balls

Have you ever eaten yams? Try these fufu balls made with mashed yams. They are very popular in Ghana.

## You will need:

- 2 pounds of yams
- ¼ teaspoon of black pepper
- 1 teaspoon of butter

## What to do:

1. Ask an adult to boil the yams in water for about 25 minutes, or until the yams are soft.
2. When the yams are cool, you can help peel off the skin.
3. Mash the yams with a wooden spoon until they are smooth.
4. Add the butter and black pepper to the mash.
5. Use your hands to roll the mash into balls.

# Celebrating Thanksgiving

Many people in the United States celebrate Thanksgiving. Pilgrims and Native Americans shared a harvest feast in 1621. Today, some people think of this feast as the first Thanksgiving.

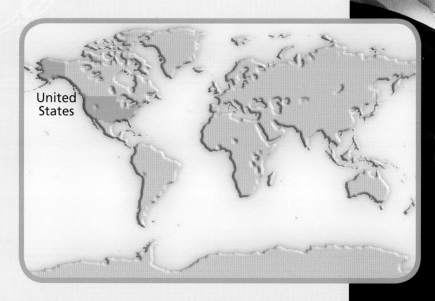

United States

Long ago, a harvest feast was shared by Pilgrims and Native Wampanoag People.

Many people eat a large meal to celebrate Thanksgiving. Turkey, potatoes, and pumpkin pie are often part of the meal. The foods we eat on Thanksgiving today are different from those served at the Pilgrims' feast. But both are celebrations of food and people.

People share a large meal to celebrate Thanksgiving.

# Pumpkin Pie

This is an easy version of this traditional Thanksgiving treat.

## You will need:

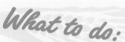

- 2 eggs
- 1 can of sweetened condensed milk
- 1 can of pumpkin
- ¼ teaspoon of cloves
- ½ teaspoon of salt
- ½ teaspoon of ginger
- 1 teaspoon of cinnamon
- ½ teaspoon of vanilla
- 1 unbaked pie shell

## What to do:

1. Beat the eggs with a fork.
2. Add all the other ingredients.
3. Stir the mixture with a wooden spoon until it is smooth.
4. Pour the mixture into the unbaked pie shell.
5. Have an adult bake the pie at 400 degrees Fahrenheit for 50 minutes, or until a toothpick stuck in the middle of the pie comes out clean.

# Harvest Festivals Around the World

People all around the world celebrate good crops. Do you have a local harvest festival? Here are some other harvest festivals that are celebrated in Asia.

Pakistan

People in Indonesia celebrate the rice harvest with a special dance.

In Vietnam, a man gives thanks during a harvest ceremony.

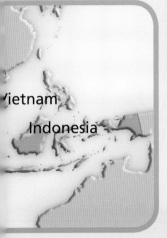

Vietnam

Indonesia

Men celebrate the harvest in Pakistan by sharing plates of bread and yak cheese.

# Index